WRITER
MARK WAID

ARTIST
CHRIS SAMNEE

COLOR ARTIST
JAVIER RODRIGUEZ

LETTERER
VC'S JOE CARAMAGNA

COVER ARTISTS
PAOLO RIVERA (#22)
CHRIS SAMNEE &
JAVIER RODRIGUEZ (#23-27)

ASSISTANT EDITOR
ELLIE PYLE

EDITOR
STEPHEN WACKER

COLLECTION EDITOR & DESIGN *CORY LEVINE*
ASSOCIATE MANAGING EDITOR *ALEX STARBUCK*
EDITORS, SPECIAL PROJECTS *JENNIFER GRÜNWALD & MARK D. BEAZLEY*
SENIOR EDITOR, SPECIAL PROJECTS *JEFF YOUNGQUIST*
SVP PRINT, SALES & MARKETING *DAVID GABRIEL*

EDITOR IN CHIEF *AXEL ALONSO*
CHIEF CREATIVE OFFICER *JOE QUESADA*
PUBLISHER *DAN BUCKLEY*
EXECUTIVE PRODUCER *ALAN FINE*

BATTLIN' JACK MURDOCK WANTED HIS SON TO LIVE HIS LIFE WITHOUT FEAR.

HE URGED MATT NOT TO FOLLOW IN HIS FOOTSTEPS AS A SMALL-TIME BOXER... TO HAVE THE GUTS TO MAKE SOMETHING OF HIMSELF.

WHEN MATT WAS STILL A TEENAGER, HE SAVED AN OLD MAN ABOUT TO BE RUN OVER BY A RUNAWAY TRUCK.

BUT A RADIOACTIVE CYLINDER FELL FROM THE TRUCK AND BLINDED MATT FOR LIFE.

YET HE SOON REALIZED HIS OTHER SENSES HAD BECOME SUPERHUMANLY ACUTE!

HE COULD TELL WHETHER OR NOT SOMEONE WAS LYING BY LISTENING TO THE PERSON'S HEARTBEAT.

HE COULD RECOGNIZE PEOPLE BY SCENT ALONE.

AND HE HAD DEVELOPED A SIXTH SENSE, A RADAR-LIKE AWARENESS OF WHERE OBJECTS WERE.

MURDOCK DIDN'T NEED ANY SUPER-POWERS TO GRADUATE AT THE TOP OF HIS LAW SCHOOL CLASS.

HE BECAME A SUCCESSFUL ATTORNEY, FULFILLING THE DREAMS OF HIS FATHER.

BATTLIN' JACK DID NOT LIVE LONG ENOUGH TO SAVOR MATT'S SUCCESS.

GANGSTERS' BULLETS CUT HIM DOWN AFTER REFUSING TO THROW A FIGHT.

JACK DIDN'T WANT MATT TO BECOME A FIGHTER. BUT TO BRING HIS FATHER'S KILLERS TO JUSTICE, HE BECAME A MAN WITHOUT FEAR.

HERE COMES...

DAREDEVIL

This page by:
Fred Van Lente, Marcos Martin,
and Blambot's Nate Piekos

TWENTY-TWO

Being blind, here are my answers to people's questions about how I handle *money*.

Yes, it's a pain that American paper currency is of a uniform size regardless of denomination.

Used to be, because of my enhanced super-senses, I could easily "read" a bill by touch.

But each advance in printing and anti-counterfeiting technology makes that more difficult.

There are smart-phone apps that can identify bills through photography. Slow, but helpful.

TEN DOLLARS.

To make better time, I still rely on the old folding method.

Ones flat...

...fins folded crosswise...

...sawbucks lengthwise...

...twenties quartered.

You have to trust cashiers not to shortchange you...

...AND TEN MAKES A HUNDRED.

...especially on *purpose*.

ARE YOU SURE?

YOU CALLIN' ME A CROOK?

NO, NO, NO.

HEY!

Tink

WE'RE EVEN.

But my most helpful tip: surrender to the 21st century and use a *debit card* as much as possible.

It's always good to have a little cash in your pocket, but the debit card is the blind man's best friend.

THIS ATM PROVIDES SPOKEN INSTRUCTIONS FOR YOUR CONVENIENCE.

TIK TAK

Withdraw $20

Transaction not processed

Please remove card

YOU HAVE EXCEEDED YOUR ACCOUNT BALANCE. PLEASE TRY AGAIN.

Except when it *isn't.*

≶SIGH≶

It's official: I'm broke. Cash-poor and *unemployed.*

The law firm of Matt Murdock and Franklin "Foggy" Nelson has *disbanded*--at first because Foggy mistakenly thought I'd been *lying* to him--

--then because I stormed out *angry.*

I'm not *destitute*-- I own my townhouse, I have no debt--

--and the celebrity crimefighter with the worst-kept secret identity can always find enough largesse to keep a body fed.

EAT, MR. DAREDEVIL!

HOW YOU LIKE THE PASTA, EH?

BELLISSIMO, LUIGI, AS ALWAYS! BUT YOU *"UNDERSTAND"* I AM *NOT* DAREDEVIL, YES? I *MUST* PAY.

SI, SIGNORE! I *"UNDERSTAND"*! STILL, I CANNOT ACCEPT PAYMENT FOR SUCH A HUMBLE MEAL FROM A MAN WHO HAS DONE SO MUCH FOR NEW YORK!

FORMAGGIO!

FORMAGGIO.

STOP! YOU'RE ONLY MAKING THIS *HARDER!*

ON *YOU,* I HOPE!

WHATEVER THIS IS, CAN WE *PLEASE* AT LEAST *TRY* NOT TO *REMIND* *RANDOM* PASSERSBY WHO I *AM?*

Where is *this* coming from? That *is Spider-Man,* right?

Pretty *sure.* The *voice* tracks, and *no one* has that same gangly-ass *posture.*

What's *off-putting* is that I'm hearing something *totally uncharacteristic* in his presence:

Silence.

BETTER. NOW, IF YOU'LL *EXPLAIN* YOURSELF--

YOU'RE A PUBLIC MENACE.

I'VE BEEN ASKED TO BRING YOU *IN*.

THAT'S ALL THE EXPLANATION YOU *REQUIRE*.

Really *not*.

I don't know what *any* of what he just said means.

NOW I'm wondering if this isn't some *mind-control* thing, because...

"...THE DIE IS CAST"? WHO TALKS LIKE THAT? WHERE DID THE FUNNY GO?

I...

...WHAT, HARD OF HEARING, TOO? I'M FULLA WISECRACKS, HORNEDHEAD!

"HORNHEAD"! IT'S "HORN--"

Okay. It's his *heartbeat*, his *scent*, his *footfall*. Legit.

Unless he's running some *elaborate prank*, Spider-Man is forcing a *fight*.

So I'm about to have to *throw down* with (sadly) the one Avenger I'm *closest* to--

--unless-- *unless*--

--I can *save* this friendship with a *magic* combination of *four words* that have never, *ever* been spoken in *any language* in this order before:

I'LL SAY.

NET!

NET!

Spontaneous acid test, Spidey: once and for all, are you *friend* or *foe?*

WHAAM!

SPIDEY! NET! NET!

NET!

Whew.

Thank you.

WAIT, *WAIT*. "I'VE BEEN ASKED TO BRING YOU IN." NOT BY THE D.A.'S OFFICE...?

ASSISTANT D.A. MCDUF--

OKAY, *NOW* YOU MAKE SENSE. I AM *HAPPY* TO EXPLAIN ONCE WE DEAL WITH *TALL BOY.*

THE ONLY ENEMY I HAVE WHO'D BUILD A TEN MILLION DOLLAR *SUIT* TO STEAL A HALF-MILLION IN *BONDS.*

... HE DIDN'T *BUILD* THIS. NOT THE *UPGRADE.* I RECOGNIZE THE *CRAFTSMANSHIP.*

HE *REPURPOSED* SOME OF M--

--SOME OF *DR. OCTOPUS'S* OLD *ARMS* INTO HIS HYDRAULICS.

DOC OCK? *THAT* TUB OF LARD?

WHY ARE YOU GRINDING YOUR TEETH?

I WAS JUST GOING TO SAY, "HE'S NOT *BEHIND* THIS, IS HE?"

HARDLY.

WHO ARE *YOU* TO CO-OPT ANOTHER MAN'S *CREATIONS*, YOU *CHARLATAN*? YOU *BABOON*? YOU'RE NOTHING BUT A *MENIAL THIEF*--

--HNNGH!

SO? YOU COME *WINDMILLING* YOUR ARMS AT *ME*, I'LL RETURN THE *FAVOR*! I KNOW YOU'RE *STRONG*, BUT *NOW*--

--SO AM *I*!

PPAAGGH!

Headstrong as *ever*. And coming from *me*--

How do I shut this *down*? Even *if* I can get him to drop *Spidey*, how can I stop him from popping *my* limbs, *too*?

By picking the perfect *strike zone*.

NO! WHAT DID YOU--? THE CENTRAL CONTROL--!

HOW DID YOU KNOW EXACTLY WHERE IT WAS?

I HAVE AUTO-SEALANT! IT'LL STEM THE DAMAGE--

TOO LATE.

KRSSSH

While Spidey shucks the unconscious *Stiltless-Man* from his now-inert *suit*, I find a *cop* and have him radio in for airlift to the *impound yard.*

Then I make *nice.*

...BREATHE LIKE I SHOWED YOU AND YOU WON'T HAVE TO BRACE. READY?

YES.

POP

¿GNNGH!¿

GO EASY FOR A FEW DAYS. ALSO, I'M *NOT* A WANTED MAN. NOR AM I A MENTALLY UNSTABLE *THREAT.*

KIRSTEN'S MY...WELL...WE'RE *CLOSE.* YOU JUST GOT DRAWN INTO A *THING* BETWEEN US.

I KEPT MY DISTANCE AT A TIME WHEN I COULD HAVE ASKED FOR HER HELP. I CONVINCED MYSELF THAT THE LACK OF COMMUNICATION WAS TO PROTECT HER, BUT THAT'S CRAP.

SHE WAS JUST THE VICTIM OF MY WORST HABIT.

YOUR LACKLUSTER FIGHTING SKILLS?

NOW HE BRINGS THE FUNNY.

I DIDN'T SHARE, FOGGY THOUGHT I'D CRACKED UP, HE TOLD KIRSTEN, AND IN THE ABSENCE OF NEWS DIRECTLY FROM ME, ETC., ETC., IT'S A MESS.

SOUNDS LIKE.

SO... GOOD?

WE'RE GOOD.

NO, I MEANT YOU, SPECIFICALLY. YOU DIDN'T SEEM YOURSELF EARLIER. ANYTHING YOU WANT TO TALK ABOUT?

...

NO. I'M FINE.*

*FINE? AS SUPERIOR SPIDER-MAN READERS KNOW, THIS IS DR. OCTOPUS IN SPIDER-MAN'S BODY, TRYING TO BE A HERO! FOLLOW SUPERIOR TO SEE IF HE SUCCEEDS!--SWACKER.

WELL, CALL IF YOU CHANGE YOUR MIND. AND THANKS FOR HELPING ME SORT THIS NONSENSE OUT. IF ANYONE NEEDS ME...

"...I NEED TO GO INVEST MY LAST TWENTY DOLLARS IN AN *APOLOGY*."

Rose's FLORIST

MA & PA BAKERY • 26

BAKERY

COOKIES
CAKES
CROISSANTS
BAGUETTES

THAT BAKERY OVER ON *CANAL*. YOU *REMEMBERED* THEIR *GREATEST CREATION*.

THE BACON AND LIMBURGER *CHEESECAKE*. IT'S MY *FAVORITE*.

OF *COURSE* IT IS. THEY *CALL* IT "THE FOGGY."

I FIGURE YOU CAN'T STOP ME FROM *TALKING* WHILE YOU'RE *HOOVERING* YOUR FOOD, SO LET ME EXPLAIN, WITHOUT INTERRUPTION, WHAT I'VE COME TO DECIDE IS THE ROOT OF OUR CONFLICT:

EVEN WHEN I WAS FIRST BLINDED, I NEVER TOLD ANYONE ABOUT MY *RADAR* OR MY *HYPERSENSES*. NOT EVEN MY *DAD*. I *ENJOYED* HAVING A BIG SECRET.

WHEN PEOPLE MAKE YOU FEEL LIKE YOU'RE *WEAK* AND HELPLESS, IT'S *EMPOWERING* TO KNOW SOMETHING THEY DON'T. AND, BOY, DID I NEED EMPOWERING.

OM NOM NOM

BACK THEN.

BACK *THEN*.

SURE THI-- WAIT.

GO BACK TO THE *PREVIOUS* QUESTION. WHAT DO YOU MEAN, *"IF THERE'S TIME"*?

And why is your heartbeat *soaring*?

AND WHY IS YOUR HEARTBEAT *SOARING*?

MATTY, I WASN'T FAIR TO YOU, EITHER.

I THINK THE REASON I WAS SO *ANGRY* THAT YOU MIGHT NOT BE DEALING WITH YOUR PROBLEMS HONESTLY AND WITH *COURAGE* IS BECAUSE I...

...I *NEED* THAT FROM YOU RIGHT NOW.

I NEED YOU TO BE THE ONE WHO CAN TEACH *ME* HOW TO DO ALL THAT.

FOGGY, WHAT ARE YOU TALKING ABOUT, PLEASE?

I'VE...BEEN SICK, MATTY. WHILE YOU'VE BEEN RUNNING AROUND, I'VE BEEN RUNNING TO THE *DOCTORS*. AND THEY'RE PRETTY SURE--

OF *WHAT?*

--THEY'RE RUNNING TESTS RIGHT NOW--

FOR WHAT, FOGGY?

...CANCER.

TWENTY-THREE

My name is *Matt Murdock.*

Brooklyn-born and raised. A bookworm as a boy. Other kids called me *"Daredevil"* because I was so timid and cautious.

Until the one time I *wasn't.*

A blind man was crossing the street--

--at the same time a *truck driver* was distracted by his *cellphone.*

I yelled at the man. Deaf, too, it turns out.

So I bolted towards him, jet-fueled by years of pent-up *fighting spirit*--

--and I slammed him out of the truck's *path*.

SKREEEE

That's when the driver opted to finally look *up*.

His tires screaming, his cargo tumbled *loose*. It had been secured with the same kind of care one would expect--

EEEE

--from a fly-by-night company that thought it'd be okay to illegally transport *toxic waste* through *New York* traffic.

Radioactive *glow* was the last thing I ever saw.

I was blinded instantly.

AHHHHH! MY EYES! IT'S IN MY EYES--!

...IT *BURNS*...!

SOMEBODY *HELP* HIM! CLEAN HIM *UP!*

I'M NOT TOUCHING THAT STUFF!

But there were... *compensations.*

The *radioactivity* gradually rewired my remaining senses... *amplified* them.

In time, I'd be able to hear *ultrafrequencies* and *heartbeats.* Read *newsprint* by *touch.*

Taste the exact number of salt grains on a *pretzel.* And *more.*

STAND BACK.

...OH, GOD, IT HURTS... IT *HUR*-- ?KGGH-GH?--

All because of a unique combination of factors. The amount of radiation I was exposed to. The speed with which it hit me.

The particulars of my own *body* chemistry.

--?K

DAMN IT.

If any of those variables had been *different,* what would have become of me then?

Tonight, Foggy Nelson wants to spit in fear's face, and I can't blame him one bit.

Apparently, he's been having headaches and joint pains for a while. Weird bruisings. Fatigue. Swellings.

In about twelve hours, I'm taking him in for the results of his blood tests--

--because his symptoms are consistent with several forms of cancer.

And other conditions. Many other eminently curable conditions.

Prepare for the worst, but hope for the best. That's my motto.

Okay, not really. But it is tonight.

REMEMBER HOW WE USED TO WAIT FOR TEST RESULTS BACK IN LAW SCHOOL?

BY STARING AT THE CLOCK?

WE'VE COME A LONG WAY.

LET'S TALK ABOUT YOUR PROBLEMS.

ME? I'M FINE.

"FINE" IS YOUR CODEWORD FOR "I DON'T WANNA TALK."

IS IT *KIRSTEN?* I SPOKE WITH HER AGAIN. SHE KNOWS I WAS OVERREACTING WHEN I TOLD HER YOU WERE INSANE.

SO SHE'S TAKING *YOUR* CALLS. *THAT'S* DUCKY.

EHHHH...IT'S JUST AS WELL. RIGHT NOW, SHE DOESN'T NEED TO BE IN THE CROSSFIRE.

OF?

BEFORE I BEAT HIM, COYOTE CONFESSED SOMETHING: I AM A MARKED MAN.

SOMEONE SPECIFIC HAS BEEN BEHIND A LOT OF MY TROUBLES SINCE I CAME BACK TO NEW YORK.

BEHIND *KLAW,* BEHIND *COYOTE* AND PROBABLY *BLACK SPECTRE,* BEHIND ATTACKS I DON'T EVEN *KNOW* ABOUT YET.

SOMEBODY'S DRAWING A *NOOSE* AROUND MY NECK. BUT WHO?

WHAT?

COULD... COULD IT BE...?

SPIT IT OUT!

THINK ABOUT IT, MATT. IT'S *OBVIOUS.* WHICH ONE OF YOUR ENEMIES HAS COME OUT OF THE WOODWORK LATELY AFTER YEARS OF OBSCURITY...

...THE LAST ONE YOU'D EXPECT. MATT, I KNOW WHO THE MASTERMIND IS WHO'S AFTER YOU.

IT'S STILT-MAN.

BWAH ha ha ha ha

"NICE-- ≥SNFF≤"

"--NICE WORK, STILT-MAN."

"YOU SHOULDN'T HAVE *SIGNED* IT."

OH, GOD.

I'M AFRAID YOUR EVIDENCE IS *LACKING*, COUNSELOR--

UH-OH. YOU HEAR THAT?

HEAR WHAT?

TROUBLE.

HELP!

HELP!

SOMEBODY!

PLEASE!

WHAT CAN I DO?

STAY SAFE! I'LL CHECK IN WHEN I'M DONE!

APPOINTMENT'S AT *NINE*--!

I KNOW, PAL! I'LL BE THERE!

TRUST ME!

Romonico Tower. Is this the 12th? I got invited to some black-tie *fundraiser* for Ron Romonico's *mayoral bid,* which Matt Murdock would have *attended*--

--if Romonico weren't an elitist *thug.* Still, haute cuisine and beautiful women...

...no wonder someone's elected to crash the party!

KRRAK

That gives the *enemy* every advantage.

For me, being in closed quarters this loud is like trying to concentrate inside a *cement mixer.*

Hard to count the attackers. They're wilding like *mindless animals.* So many noises, so much motion, so many...

Terrific. Utter *chaos.*

≥ SNFF ≥

...*smells*...what is *that* one? It's *familiar,* but where do I--

HNNGHH!

St... strong... wow...

Makes it a tougher *fight*, adrenaline. The air's *thick* with the odor. It's amping their muscles and deadening their *reactions*.

Can't *shake* this one--

RAAAGGH!

AAAAAIEE!

AAAANNGHH

GHAAAHH!

Holding his +hnnggh!+

--his *ear* in *pain?* Why--?

Wait. That *stench*. It's positively *rancid* on these guys--

--and while I smelled it only *once*, over *twenty* years ago--

--there's no way I could ever *forget* it.

My God. Oh, my *God*.

It's the toxin that BLINDED ME.

No wonder they're berserk. Whoever *did* this to these poor bastards must have set them *loose* in the *city*--where their *hypersenses* would drive them *insane!*

I recall what it was *like* that first day, to be overwhelmed to the point of *madness.*

AAAIIEE!

The slightest *pain* was *incapacitating.*

That's half the gang. The *other* half--

--I'm going to have to *catch.*

TIK

A M

This is a threat *tailored* to me. Whoever's out to get me has pulled his sickest stunt *yet*.

SIR, GET *BACK IN THE STORE!*

I'LL HANDLE TH--

He *ducked?*

Of *course* he ducked, dummy.

He's got radar sense, *too!*

KRSSHH

SORRY, CLO

TASE
HIM!
HURRY!

That's
one.

I SAID,
FREEZE!
DO IT!

DON'T
MAKE US
SHOOT YOU,
MAN!

TWO.

9:0

BZZZT
Incoming Tex
Matt

Hey, buddy--

HI, MR. NELSON. I SEE YOU BROUGHT A FRIEND.

WELL, HE HAS A THING FOR NURSES.

AH.

ONE SECOND. LET ME JUST CHECK THE LAST OF THESE RESULTS...

It's gonna be okay.

It's gonna be fine. I can read the doctor. I can feel it.

Poor Foggy, though. He's trying to play it cool, but his heartbeat's so loud, I don't even *recognize* it. It's--

It's not Foggy's.

I'M
SORRY.

WELL, I THINK IT'S ALL COMING TOGETHER NICELY.

SURELY--HE--SUSPECTS...

WHICH--CREATES--ITS--OWN--MYSTERY...

EXCLUSIVE
Milla Donovan
wife of
DARE DEVIL

24 TIPS TO TAME YOUR MANE

Is your ma__ leading a double life?

I DON'T FOLLOW.

The REVEALER
LATE EDITION • 25 CE__

SAVAGE WILDERS ATTACK CITY

VILLAIN SPO_
KIDNAPP_
FROM
CUSTO_

YOU SENT KLAW. COYOTE. THE WILDERS.

MORE THAT HE'S LIKELY UNAWARE OF.

COYOTE'S SCHEM__
UNEARTHE__

LOCAL INTEREST

DAILY BUGLE
KLAW CREATUR_
ON THE LOOS_

The REVEALER
MEGACRIME
_ES EXPOSED

MEMORIAL SLOAN-KETTERING CANCER CENTER.

YORK AVE, NEW YORK, NY.

I hate hospitals. I hate the smell of meds, I hate the taste of the air, and I hate the bustle. Four A.M. and it's like trying to concentrate in Grand Central Station during morning rush.

But I will stay.

NURSE? NURSE!

...PAGING DR. ANSELMO...

And I will try not to overthink.

I'm the one who took a faceful of *radioactive waste* when I was a kid.

And yet, it's my *best friend* who got hit with *cancer.*

How is *that* fair?

They're doing an invasive biopsy tomorrow so they can determine how aggressive to make the *chemo.*

STOP THAT MAN

Cytotoxins. Podophyllotoxins. Everything ends with "toxins."

HE'S RAIDED THE PHARMACY STOP HIM

And even though Foggy hasn't put anything healthy in his body since he accidentally ate that *apple* in 1998--

--that's still going to be *rough* on him.

HNNNNH!

TOK

CLUMSY IDIOT.

WOW... YOU'RE THAT *DESPERATE,* ARE YOU?

I'M *FINE.*

STOP. SITTING STILL IS *KILLING* YOU. YOU'RE *DYING* FOR ACTION.

STOP *HOVERING.* I'M *GOOD.* GO FIGHT *ELECTRO* OR SOMETHING.

CITY CAN DO WITHOUT *DAREDEVIL* A LITTLE LONGER.

THEN GO TALK TO *KIRSTEN.*

I'D RATHER FIGHT *ELECTRO.*

GO.

Kirsten McDuffie is an assistant district attorney. We've been dating.

Then she tried to have me arrested.

Seems like a good time to break it off.

I'll let her down easy.

YOUR SECRETARY SAID YOU WERE HERE.

WHAT DID YOU HAVE TO OFFER HER?

A SIGNED PICTURE OF THOR.

HEY!

YOU! NO ONE'S ALLOWED TO CLIMB WITHOUT A SAFETY HARNESS! DIDN'T YOU READ THE RULES?

I'M BLIND! NO WORRIES!

GET DOWN FROM THERE!

STAFF

DID FOGGY CALL YOU?

HE DID. HE EXPLAINED WHY HE THOUGHT YOU'D GONE CRAZY. SOMETHING ABOUT A SUPER-VILLAIN PLOT.

AND YOU CALLED IN SPIDER-MAN TO COLLAR ME AS A MISINFORMED MATTER OF PUBLIC SAFETY?

AND FOR YOUR OWN GOOD.

THAT'S WEIRDLY SWEET.

CAN WE NOT TALK ABOUT THIS RIGHT NOW?

WHY NOT?

BECAUSE I'M ON A *DATE*.

What a relief. That actually takes all the angst out of my closing argument.

No hearts to break, no "*It's not you, it's me.*" We're on the same page, and we can simply move on like two mature adults.

JUST GIVE ME TWO MINUTES OF YOUR TIME.

WUMP

JAKE, I NEED A MOMENT WITH THE BLIND GUY.

MATT, MEET JAKE.

COLUMBIA

THIS IS YOUR *DATE?*

I THOUGHT HE WAS PART OF THE ROCK WALL.

AMUSING.

WE WON'T BE LONG.

I DECIDED YOU AND I SHOULDN'T BE A COUPLE.

THAT IS NOT UNWISE. MY ENEMIES LIKE TO TARGET THOSE CLOSE TO ME.

THAT'S NOT WHY, HUMBLE-BRAG.

I'M NOT ANKLING BECAUSE I'M AFRAID OF BEING A *TARGET.*

I'M DISENGAGING BECAUSE YOU HAVE BIG, *OPERATIC* ENEMIES THAT ARE A PART OF DAREDEVIL'S BIG, OPERATIC *LIFE.*

IT IS A BIG LIFE.

AND BECAUSE OF THAT, I WAS SKATING THE EDGE OF BEING KNOWN NOT AS "KIRSTEN McDUFFIE, OUR NEWEST D.A.," OR "KIRSTEN McDUFFIE, LEGAL EAGLE"...

...BUT "KIRSTEN McDUFFIE, DAREDEVIL'S *GIRLFRIEND.*"

YOU ARE A LARGER-THAN-LIFE FIGURE, MY FRIEND.

THAT'S TRUE.

I DON'T FAULT YOU. YOU CAN'T HELP BUT OVERSHADOW PRETTY MUCH *ANYBODY* YOU STAND NEXT TO.

BUT I CAN'T BE A SUPPORTING PLAYER IN *"THE ADVENTURES OF DAREDEVIL."* I NEED TO BE THE STAR OF MY *OWN* LIFE.

BE WELL, MATT.

Oh, my God.

I think I'm in *love* with this woman.

Starving for *something* to break in my direction, I follow a neglected lead.

HANK? MATT. YOU GOT ANYTHING FOR ME?

Hank Pym is an Avenger who's mastered size control.

HOLD ON. I'M IN THE MIDDLE OF SOMETHING.

STOP SHOUTING.

That's because he's a brilliant biochemist--which made him my natural *go-to.*

SORRY.

OKAY, I DID MY OWN EXAMINATION ON THOSE *BLIND CONVICTS* YOU CAUGHT A COUPLE OF WEEKS AGO.

YOU WERE *ABSOLUTELY* RIGHT. THEY ALL SHOWED TRACES OF RADIATION CLOSE IF NOT *IDENTICAL* TO THE READINGS I FOUND INSIDE YOUR NERVOUS SYSTEM.*

*ISSUE 16-- GIANT-WACKER.

SO SOMEONE'S REPLICATED THE CHEMICAL BATH THAT BLINDED ME.

IT WOULD SEEM.

... ANYTHING *RARE* IN THE INGREDIENTS?

LOOK! IT'S SPIDER-MAN!

THAT'S WHAT I'M TRYING TO FIND OUT.

FIRST, I HAVE TO *RETRO-ENGINEER* THE BLOOD AND SKIN SAMPLES I TOOK OFF THE CONVICTS TO FIND THE "RECIPE."

NOW YOU SOUND LIKE A *CARTOON MOUSE.*

Murdock
00:01:57

SORRY SORRY.

AH. THERE YOU ARE...

WITH THAT IN HAND, I CAN MAYBE--*MAYBE*--MATCH SOME OF IT AGAINST *PURCHASE ORDERS* TO FIND A *BUYER.*

IN OTHER NEWS, HOW'S *FOGGY?*

WE'RE NOT SURE. THE DOCTORS ARE HAVING A TOUGH TIME *DIAGNOSING.*

WHATEVER IT IS, IT'S CENTERED IN HIS PELVIS AND RIGHT FEMUR.

AND THEY'VE RULED OUT YOUR *STANDARD* LYMPHOMAS? OSTEOMYELITIS? OSTEOSARCOMA?

THEY'RE THINKING MAYBE THOSE LAST TWO, BUT...

HMM.

WHAT?

JUST RUNNING OVER THE SYMPTOMS YOU MENTIONED... HEY, MATT?

ASK HIS DOCTOR IF HE'S A *GIANTS* FAN.

EWING'S SARCOMA.

A BONE TUMOR THAT FAVORS THE *TORSO*. EASY TO MISTAKE BECAUSE IT'S VERY *RARE* IN FULL ADULTS.

IT SOUNDS FAMILIAR. WHY HAVE I HEARD OF IT?

IT WAS PART OF LAST YEAR'S *SUPER BOWL* COVERAGE. GIANTS LINEBACKER *MARK HERZLICH* OVERCAME EWING'S TO PLAY IN THE BIG GAME.

RIGHT. YEAH. OKAY. WELL...

...IF A *TOP ATHLETE* IN *PEAK PHYSICAL CONDITION* CAN BEAT THIS, THEN IT SHOULD BE A *SNAP* FOR *ME*, HUH?

STAY POSITIVE.

TALK TO US ABOUT ODDS, DOC.

BETWEEN CHEMO, RADIATION AND SURGERY, SURVIVAL RATES ARE NEAR 70% IF, LIKE HERZLICH'S, THE CANCER HASN'T METASTASIZED.

THAT'S WHAT WE'RE TRYING TO DETERMINE NOW-- IF IT'S SPREAD.

AND IF IT HAS?

LET'S NOT--

IF. IT. HAS?

CLOSER TO 10%.

At Foggy's insistence, I stop by the office to make sure the trains are running on time.

We both know that's like asking a six-year-old to balance the checkbook, but desperate times, etc.

AFTERNOON, ALYSSA. WHO CALLED WHILE I WAS OUT?

EVERYONE.

SWELL.

The good news is, my private client has made his monthly retainer payment, and that keeps the lights on.

I should tell Foggy about that arrangement, but I'm not in the mood to be *yelled* at for taking on the case of *ten lifetimes* against--

KNOCK KNOCK

MR. MURDOCK? THERE'S A DELIVERY FOR YOU UP FRONT.

PRETTY BIG CRATE.

SNFF

SNIFF SNIFF

You test on animals.

GRR WAAR AAF RI RRR

EVERYONE OUT! GO! GO!

SWAK

Too much commotion.

Can't get my bearings.

As far as my radar sense goes, I might as well be in a tornado.

FIRE

BRAAATT BRAAATTBRAAAT

A nerve pinch taught to me by *Iron Fist* knocks the dogs unconscious...

...and an *Avenger* can take it from there.

HANK? ME AGAIN.

I NEED ANOTHER *FAVOR*...

While I wait for my ad hoc clean-up crew, I call all our employees to check on them.

No one got bit, but I ask them all to get checked regardless, even if it's just for post-traumatic stress--

--and work from home until I can erase this *target* from my back.

Like Kirsten said...I have an operatic life.

THERE. I'LL TAKE THEM BACK TO MY LAB FOR TREATMENT AND STUDY.

MUCH APPRECIATED, HANK. NEXT TIME YOU NEED A LAWYER, REMEMBER THE WORDS "PRO" AND "BONO."

WHOEVER'S BEHIND THIS IS TURNING THE SCREWS FASTER NOW. WHAT ELSE CAN I DO TO HELP?

JUST GET ME A LINE ON THOSE CHEMICALS.

ALSO, IF YOU COULD WHIP UP A CURE FOR *EWING'S SARCOMA*...

SOME THINGS ARE BEYOND ALL OUR POWERS, AREN'T THEY?

I'LL BE IN TOUCH.

Who *is* turning the screws?

Who **have** I ticked off enough in my career to come at me this methodically?

I start to go down the list.

By the time I hit the "B"s, I've been in Foggy's room an hour, but I can't surrender the challenge.

What if whoever's doing this decided to go after *him* next? He's not exactly in any condition to fight *back*.

Nor should he *need* to be.

Being my friend shouldn't have to come at a *cost*.

TEACH ME, MATT.

TEACH YOU WHAT?

HOW TO BE LIKE YOU. HOW TO BE A MAN WITHOUT *FEAR*.

YOU HAVEN'T ABANDONED ME EVEN THOUGH HALF THE *UNDERWORLD* KNOWS DAREDEVIL'S REAL NAME AND WHERE HE WORKS?

YEAH.

EVEN THOUGH I'M A MAGNET FOR TROUBLE AND YOU'RE A BOX OF *IRON FILINGS*?

I GUESS.

SOUNDS TO ME LIKE YOU ALREADY *ARE A MAN WITHOUT FEAR*, BUDDY.

So keep *thinking*, Matty. Who's grinding this particular axe?

C'mon...just one stinking clue...one tiny thread to follow...just *one*...

MATT MURDOCK?

TWENTY-FIVE

By the time I give Larry a top-of-the-Brooklyn-Bridge view of the East River, he starts breathing normally.

OH, MY GOD, HOW DO YOU GET YOUR BEARINGS *SWINGIN'* LIKE THIS? I CAN'T SEE *ANYTHING!*

OH. RIGHT.

THAT'S THE PLACE. RIGHT THERE.

UH-HUH. ALL RIGHT. NOW, GET YOUR ASS TO THE CORNER OF *HICKS* AND *AMITY.* THERE'S AN E.R. THERE.

CHECK YOURSELF *IN* AND TELL THEM TO OPERATE *FAST.*

OP-OPERATE--?

WHAT AM I, AN *IDIOT?* I *KNOW* YOU WERE *SUPPOSED* TO BRING ME HERE, KID!

YOU ARE THE MOST *CONVENIENTLY TIMED* "LUCKY *BREAK"* IN *HISTORY*...!

THEY *DIDN'T* WANT ME TO *KNOW* YOU WERE *LYING,* LARRY! DEAR GOD--

HANG ON.

"--THAT'S *WHY* THEY GAVE YOU A *PACEMAKER."*

IT'S ALMOST *CERTAINLY SABOTAGED,* SO GO OR I TAKE YOU! IT HAS TO COME *OUT* BEFORE--

SHK

Ah, hell.

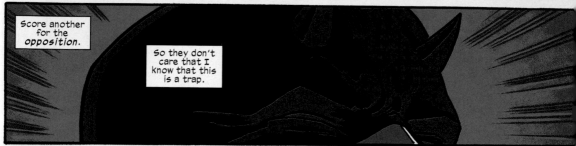

Score another for the *opposition*.

So they don't care that I know that this is a trap.

And it's a good one. I hear *nothing* from inside.

Smell nothing.

Taste *nothing* on the air.

If that's supposed to freak me out, whoever's beneath this roof doesn't know me at all.

TIK

I don't scare.

Bare to the walls. Utterly *empty.*

Nothing *hidden?* Could I have been *wrong* about--

YOU'RE HERE.

GOOD.

LARRY WAS TELLING THE TRUTH ABOUT ONE THING, MR. MURDOCK.

CRNCH

SKUNCH

FFFFT

FFFFFT

CRNC
CRN

CRNCH
CRNC

RRRNCH

THERE WERE EXPERIMENTS.

SKRREEEE

HORRIBLE, *GHASTLY* EXPERIMENTS.

Toxic waste.

Old-penny smell of bloody *boxing wraps.*

The shaving cream...

Familiar *scents. Pungent.*

SKREEE CHNK

...on his *silk?*

SOMEONE *HAS,* IN FACT, MANAGED TO RE-CREATE THE TOXIC CHEMICALS THAT BLINDED YOU, GAVE YOU ENHANCED SENSES.

MURDOC[

SOMEONE WHOSE *HATE* FOR YOU KEEPS HIM *ALIVE.*

BUT HE DIDN'T *WASTE* THE PROCESS ON WEAK, MALNOURISHED *VAGRANTS.*

"HE USED IT TO BAPTIZE A *WARRIOR.*"

"A FIGHTER TRAINED TO BE EVERY BIT YOUR *EQUAL* IN SKILL--"

"--AND, NOW, IN *POWER.*"

SPECIMEN 87
Toxicity Level 12
Radiation Level 14

YOU *DARE* COME BEFORE ME WRAPPED IN THE *ROBE* OF MY *FATHER?*

WHO ARE YOU?

Which is appropriate, because I'm *pissed*.

AMATEUR. YOU CARRY YOUR *WEIGHT* LIKE A BLIND MAN. LEAVES YOU VULNERABLE IN SEVEN WAYS.

SHOW ME.

I'LL LEAVE YOU ENOUGH BREATH TO TELL ME WHO YOUR *BOSS* IS.

WH--?

TWIFF

HNGGH

WE *BOTH* HAVE *RADAR SENSE*, MR. *MURDOCK*.

Of course.

That explains the *venue*.

That's why he picked an *empty warehouse* as an arena:

Solid echoes, no clutter, no *distractions.* Perfect for a *tyro* at *sightlessness.*

He won't fare *near* as well *outside.*

This is *my* battleground.

The only thing he has going for him out here--

--is dumb luck.

Don't drag this out, Matt. Put him down *fast*--

--fast, before--

WHFF

GHAAH!

Right...to the *bone*...

...I got *cocky*... was *stupid*...

...but the *Kusurigama* blades... they're his only *trick*. Got to seize the *offensive*.

He's *wide open*, with nowhere to go but--

TIK

--down.

NO!

My *grapple hook*--!

That leaves him two weapons to my *one*.

HWUFF!

Don't get *rattled*, Matt. Don't forget, he's *new*.

You've been doing this a *lifetime*--

--and you learned from the *best*.

SWAK

ALWAYS KEEP YOUR *GUARD* UP, BOY! *ALWAYS!* HOW MANY TIMES DO I HAVE TO *TELL* YOU?

OW. I'M *CONCENTRATING*, OKAY, STICK? *GIVE* ME A SECOND!

'KAY. I UNDERSTAND.

WE'RE IN NO RUSH. WHENEVER YOU'RE READY. *RELAX.*

YOU GET *FLUSTERED*, IT CLOUDS YOUR *PERCEPTIONS.* WHAT DO YOU *"SEE"*?

LONG WAY *DOWN.*

TO WHAT?

A... *ROOFTOP*, I THINK? NO, A *CANOPY*. NO, *ROOFTOP.*

ANY LEDGES ALONG THE WAY? FLAGPOLES?

I CAN'T *TELL*. I...I CAN'T KEEP THE IMAGES *SHARP* IN MY *MIND.*

I KNOW YOU WANT ME TO *JUMP*, BUT I'M NOT *READY*, STICK. NOT YET.

THANKS FOR BEING *PATIENT* WITH ME.

UH-HUH.

YAAAAH!

God, I hated that man.

But he taught me *well*.

Now it's straight *hand-to-hand.*

We trade fifty blows.

A *hundred.*

It's rapidly becoming an *endurance* test. Same number of contusions, same *ribs* cracked.

On the one hand, I'm *down* points because I can feel my *sternum* rattling and a *concussion* trying to strangle my *brain.*

But on the other hand--

SNAP

--only *one* of us still has a telescoping *billy club.*

Score.

I can smell *sweat* and *blood* under his mask.

I can hear his aching lungs struggle for *air* and his broken bones *scrape*. He's hurting *bad*.

There's a *pain* in my chest that's getting *sharper*. If I don't *end* this in the next *minute* or so, it'll drop me.

And I'm sure he's thinking exactly the *same* about me.

But we're too evenly matched to keep *brawling*. It's time to press my *sole advantage*.

He may have *radar sense* like *mine*--

--but he hasn't had a lifetime to *master* it.

I have.

Still early.

JANSON'S
PORTING GOODS

GHNNGH--!

I recall this being a *sporting goods* store. It'll be *empty*.

So far, so good.

As I predicted, he's moving haltingly.

500 COUNT MATCHES 3 for the price of 1

FLAME ON! MATCHES
FLAME ON! MATCHES
FLAME ON! MATCHES
FLAME ON! MATCHES
FLAME ON! MATCHES
FLAME ON! MATCHES

So many objects, so many shapes... his radar is overwhelmed.

SKTCH

This won't help.

PFTSSSS

I've--

--oh, God, it hurts more *not* to breathe--

--I've been praying for *years* that no one would think to use a sprinkler system on *me*.

Sense of smell, *negated.* Hearing, *nullified.*

All that leaves...

...don't black out, Matt, *don't black out...*

...all that leaves is *radar sense*, which is practically *useless* in the rain. Mine's cut 95%.

But Ikari's is completely *out.*

He's right next to me and he has no way of knowing it.

Only one shot.

Still strong enough for one good shot.

TRY THE *RED* ONE.

He's not blghhgh--➤➤

--blind--

--WHATSAMATTER, "DAREDEVIL"? SCARED? AH HA HA HA HA!

Get up, Matt!

Your dad... taught you, too...

DAD

...taught you... always...

...always... get up...

get

IT'S ALMOST OVER, MR. MURDOCK.

HKKKKKKK

ALMOST.

NOW YOU KNOW HOW YOUR LIFE WILL END.

AND BY WHOSE WILL.

WHAT WE *DON'T* WANT YOU TO KNOW IS THE *WHEN*.

IT *WILL BE SOON*. TONIGHT, PERHAPS. OR THE NEXT, AT MOONRISE. OR FIVE MINUTES FROM NOW. IT *WILL BE SOON*.

BUT I *PROMISE* YOU, YOU WILL *NEVER* SENSE IT COMING.

AND THAT *SCARES* YOU.

SADISTIC, YES. BUT YOUR PULSE IS *POUNDING*. I CAN *HEAR* IT. AND COMING FROM *YOU*, THE SOUND IS *MELODIC*.

WHAT'S THE LAST SOUND *YOU'LL* HEAR, MURDOCK? *MY* FOOTSTEPS? THE SCREECH OF *BRAKES*, THE CRACK OF A *RIFLE*? IT COULD BE ANY OF THOSE THINGS!

MY MASTER *ALONE* KNOWS HOW TO *FRIGHTEN* YOU, MURDOCK! *HE KNOWS HOW TO STAB YOUR HEART!*

RUN, MURDOCK!

RUN FOR YOUR LIFE!

TWENTY-SIX

IT'S DONE.

IS--HE-- DEAD...?

NOT YET.

SPLENDID...

YOU SHOULD HAVE SEEN HIM SCRAMBLE TO GET AWAY. LIKE A WHIPPED DOG.

AND HE DOESN'T EVEN KNOW WHO'S BEHIND THE ATTACK.

WHY WOULD HE?

AS FAR AS THE WORLD IS CONCERNED--

DON'T--SPIT--THE-- WORDS...

WHAT-- WAS--DONE-- TO--ME--WAS-- NOT--A-- SETBACK...

...BUT--A-- GIFT...

WHEN--MY--BODY--COULD--MOVE...

...COULD--FEEL...

...I--WAS--MERELY--A--WEAPON...

NOW--MY--MIND--HAS--BEEN--FREED...

...TO--DO--NOTHING--BUT--THINK--

--AND--PLOT--

--AND--PLAN...

"TO--
TARGET..."

Tonight, a man
with my powers
beat me to within
an inch of my life...

...and
I ran.

Like a
coward.

I'm glad
you're not
here to see
this, Dad.

But don't
worry.

According to
my enemy, I'll
be with you
soon enough.

"I will kill
you," Ikari
said.

But not kill
me there,
not then. Too
merciful.

He'll do it
five minutes
from now.

Or five days. Or five
hours. He wants me to
suffer first, trembling
in terror every time
I open a door or go
around a corner.

I've faced
death before,
but not in a
cold sweat.

So why is this
time different?
Why am I scared
out of my
mind? WHY--

HELLO?

IS ANYONE HERE?

I HAVE AN *INTERVIEW* APPOINTMENT...?

JUST A MINUTE!

WHAT INTERVIEW?

TO FILL IN FOR MR. NELSON...? HIS ASSISTANT CONTACTED ME ON HIS BEHALF? I FORGET THE *NAME*...

Corrine. Who, like the rest of the staff, is enjoying the *paid leave* I gave everyone after the *office* was attacked.

I'LL BE *RIGHT WITH YOU!* JUST *HANG ON!*

Or else I'd check with *her*, because I don't remember being told *about* this interview.

HAVE A SEAT, MISTER....

BENSON. LAWRENCE BENSON. HARVARD LAW, '97.

I CAN COME BACK AT A BETTER TIME...

NO SUCH THING. SIT.

YOU MUST BE *MATT MURDOCK.* I KNOW ALL ABOUT YOU.

WHAT DO YOU MEAN BY *THAT?*

NOTHING! I'VE... FOLLOWED YOUR *CAREER!*

CAN...CAN YOU TELL ME MORE ABOUT WHAT YOU'D *NEED* ME FOR?

Wouldn't Corrine have covered that in the pre-interview? Maybe. Maybe not.

MY PARTNER'S BEGINNING AGGRESSIVE TREATMENT FOR HIS CANCER. SOMEONE HAS TO ASSUME HIS...

...HIS CASELOAD...

THIS IS JUST A JOB INTERVIEW, MR. BENSON, NOT A CROSS-EXAM. WHY SO NERVOUS?

WHO, ME? I'M FINE.

A lie.

But it could be the interview.

On the other hand, Ikari promised that I could die at any moment.

CHK

Not necessarily by his direct hand.

What's in the *briefcase,* Mr. Benson...?

WHO SENT YOU?

AAAAAHH!

THWAK

Calcium smell. Unmistakable.

Not a weapon, you paranoid freak.

Antacids.

I--I HAVE TO GO--!

MR. BENSON, *WAIT!* I APOLOGIZE. I'M UNDER A LOT OF *PRESSURE...*

YOU SEEM PRETTY WORKED UP.

I AM.

GOOD. IKARI WILL BE GLAD TO HEAR THAT.

By the time I hit the lobby, "Benson" has already vanished.

Stupid. stupid. I let my *guard* dow--

BZZZT
BZZZT

∫ HNNH♪∫

Cellphone. Calm yourself.

MR. MURDOCK? THIS IS NURSE AYERS AT SLOAN-KETTERING. WE'VE BEEN TRYING TO REACH YOU--

Foggy's chemo.

It started two hours ago.

Screw the secret identity. Hospital's only a few blocks from here. Just *go*.

ONE SIDE! COMING *THROUGH!*

At least at street level, I'm reasonably *camouflaged.* I could probably make even better time as Daredevil--

--but then I'd be a *sitting duck.*

RUN, MURDOCK.

RUN.

WATCH IT!

CLUMSY IDIOT--!

WHERE'S THE *FIRE,* PAL?

FACE ME LIKE A MAN!

Cancer ward. A hundred noises, a thousand smells. A chaotic jungle where I'm not the lion.

‹EXIT›

Foggy's room. They said the anti-nauseauls would take a half-hour and the potassium/magnesium drip another two, so that makes this the actual "cocktail," but--

--I don't remember--aren't they supposed to take him to a *ward* for this?

A syringe? Why not an I.V.? Is it *supposed* to smell like that? Like--

FOGGY, HAVE YOU EVER SEEN THIS NURSE BEFORE?

I...I DUNNO...

SIR, I'M GOING TO HAVE TO ASK YOU TO NOT UPSET MR. NELSON. YOU CAN WAIT OUTSIDE.

WHAM

YOU'D LIKE THAT, WOULDN'T YOU?

MATT, WHAT THE HELL--?

HE'S HERE TO KILL YOU, FOGGY!

WHAT ARE YOU *TALKING* ABOUT? HAVE YOU GONE *INSANE?*

OH, GOD. MAYBE. I DON'T *KNOW!* I'M *SORRY!* I--

On the *label.*

"*Got you.*"

HE LEFT A *MESSAGE*, FOGGY! TO *TAUNT* ME! *BRAILLE!* FEEL IT!

MATTY?

WE'VE GOT TO GET YOU *OUT* OF HERE! COME ON!

MATT! MATT, *STOP!* WHAT HAS GOTTEN *INTO* YOU?

DO NOT GO CRAZY ON ME *NOW*, MATTY! YOU'RE ALL I'VE *GOT* RIGHT NOW, MAN! YOU'RE *IT!* YOU'RE NOT HERE TO HELP ME THROUGH THIS, I *DIE!*

SO *EXPLAIN* YOURSELF!

WHAT HAS GOT YOU SO *TERRIFIED?*

... THAT. WHAT YOU JUST SAID, THAT.

I'VE BEEN TRYING TO FIGURE OUT WHY I'M SCARED, AND THAT'S IT. IF HE KILLS ME, WHERE DOES THAT LEAVE *YOU?*

OKAY, WAIT. BACK UP. WHO'S TRYING TO KILL YOU?

TODAY?

THAT'S JUST IT. I'M NOT *SURE.* REMEMBER, I SAID SOMEONE USED *COYOTE* AGAINST ME? SOMEONE'S *CLOSING IN?*

WELL, LET'S EXAMINE THE *EVIDENCE.*

I'M TAKING NOTES. START FROM THE BEGINNING.

FIRST WAS *KLAW*. HE WAS SENT AFTER ME, BUT I NEVER FOUND OUT BY *WHO*.

BUT THAT WAS ONLY THE FIRST CIRCLE OF THIS HELL.

CIRCLE. VERY COLORFUL METAPHOR. OKAY, KLAW. NEXT?

KLAW

THEN THAT BUSINESS WITH MY FATHER'S *REMAINS* BEING HIDDEN IN MY DESK. THAT WAS CLOSER, MORE PERSONAL.

KLAW

JACK MURDOCK

IKARI

THAT WAS *COYOTE*, RIGHT?

YEAH. CIRCLES *WITHIN* CIRCLES. COYOTE *BRAGGED* THAT SOMEONE HIRED HIM TO SCREW WITH ME--BUT NOT *KILL* ME.

THAT JOB GOES TO AN ASSASSIN NAMED *IKARI*.

HE'S THE REASON I'M A PARANOID WRECK. HE'S STALKING ME.

HE CAN'T TAKE YOU.

HE *CAN!* THAT'S JUST *IT!* HE NEARLY *KILLED* ME TONIGHT, FOGGY! I'M ONLY ALIVE *NOW* BECAUSE HE WANTS TO *TORMENT* ME, AND HE *CAN!*

HE HAS ALL THE SAME *POWERS* AS ME... *AND HE CAN SEE!*

MATTY...

JUST WHEN I *FINALLY* HAVE MY LIFE WHERE I *WANT* IT...! WHO'S AT THE *CENTER* OF ALL THIS, FOGGY? *WHO MADE ME A TARGET?*

I THINK... I THINK I...

MATT, "READ" THIS.

WHAT IS THIS? YOUR GUESS?

KLAW

JACK MURDOCK

IKARI

IT CAN'T...

THIS ISN'T HIS...

...FOGGY, BULLSEYE IS *DEAD. I KILLED HIM. I STABBED HIM THROUGH THE CHEST.*

NO. YOU DID NOT.

"YOU WERE *POSSESSED*, MATTY. THAT WAS *NOT YOU*.

"NOT *THEN*, AND NOT *LATER* WHEN YOU AND THE *HAND* TRIED TO *RESURRECT* HIM! DO YOU REMEMBER *THAT*?"

IN MY NIGHTMARES. BUT THE AVENGERS *STOPPED* ME. *YOU* WERE THERE. NO. BULLSEYE'S *DEAD*. AFTER THE *FIGHT*, THE AVENGERS--

--COULDN'T FIND THE *CORPSE*.

First step: duck out of the crosshairs.

Ikari's no doubt tracking my every move the same way I would *his*:

By listening for the distinctive *heartbeat* of his *prey*.

I can't stop my pulse, nor can I mute it.

But I can *change* it.

Adrenaline.

IT'S *ME.* MURDOCK TOOK HIMSELF *OFF THE GRID.*

I DON'T *KNOW* HOW!

PROBABLY TO HIS *APARTMENT.* HIS *OFFICE.* SOMEPLACE *PRIVATE,* WITHOUT *CANNON FODDER* AROUND.

TELL ME HOW YOU WISH ME TO PROCEED.

KSSSSSHHHHH

Lady Bullseye--of *course*--martial *artist*. Normally a *threat to me* but

not
today

not
ambushed

not

KRNCHT

able
to
drop
me

KA
AK

IT IS HIM, ISN'T IT?

WHERE IS HE? WHERE IS HE HIDING--?

Wheeze of a respirator. Crackle of a voicebox and the smell of urine.

None of which disguises him.

SO THIS IS WHAT YOU'VE BECOME.

BULLSEYE, THE WORLD'S DEADLIEST MAN.

AN INVALID KEPT ALIVE BY MACHINES.

IF ALL THAT'S LEFT OF YOU IS YOUR SICK, TWISTED MIND, I CAN IMAGINE NO MORE FITTING PUNISHMENT.

I'D CALL THAT A VICTORY.

TWENTY-SEVEN

YOU GOT THE SAME CALL?

"REPORT BACK TO WORK IMMEDIATELY OR BE *FIRED*"? PRETTY *HARSH.*

I MEAN, *LOOK* AT THIS PLACE. IT'S STILL A *MESS* FROM WHEN THOSE *DOGS* ATTACKED.

SO NUT UP AND *PICK* UP. MR. MURDOCK GAVE US *PAID LEAVE* AFTER THAT. MORE'N MOST BOSSES WOULD DO.

BESIDES, HE MIGHT HEAR YOU.

MR. MURDOCK, YOU IN YOUR *OFFICE?*

MR. *MURDOCK?*

HUH.

PRIVATE

Bullseye's certain he *has* me.

If I reveal that I know *Ikari's* standing behind me, Ikari *attacks*.

If I play *dumb*, he'll attack *anyway*.

Bullseye thinks it doesn't *matter*, and he's *right*.

All that *does* matter is that a *three* foot distance...

...is less than *six*.

SSHHHNG

FREEZE.

--IF YOU SAY THAT DR. FINE ASKED YOU TO LOOK *IN* ON MR. NELSON, THAT'S WELCOME NEWS. HE'S HAVING A ROUGH NIGHT, POOR MAN.

SLOAN-KETTERING CANCER CENTER.

I'LL LEAVE YOU TO HIM, DOCTOR.

TRULY-- YOU-- DON'T.

THEN *TAUNT* ME. *REVEL* IN THIS MOMENT.

"TELL ME HOW YOU WENT FROM *MASTER ASSASSIN--*"

--TO THIS?

ONE--DOES--NOT--
ASSOCIATE--WITH--
THE--HAND--THIS--
LONG--

--AND--NOT--BENEFIT--
FROM--THEIR--
RESURRECTION--
POWERS.

LADY--BULLSEYE--
TOOK--CHARGE--OF--
THE--CEREMONY--

--BUT--NOT--EVEN--
HER--DEVOTION--
COULD--MANDATE
--MIRACLES.

"I--WAS--
ALIVE--

"--BUT--
IRREPARABLY--
DAMAGED--

"--STONE--
DEAF--

"YOU'VE--
CRIPPLED--ME--
BEFORE--

"--TOTALLY--
PARALYZED--
UTTERLY--
IMMOBILE--

"--BUT--THIS--
TIME--THE--
DAMAGE--YOU--
INFLICTED--TO--
MY--SPINE--WAS--
IRREPARABLE.

"BUT--WHILE--
MY--PROTEGE--
REBUILT--ME--

"--I--FOUND--
A--NEW--FOCUS--
FOR--MY--AGONY.

"A--NEW--
TARGET."

YOU KNOW WHO I AM. WHERE I WORK, WHERE I LIVE.

IF YOU CREATED *IKARI*, YOU EVEN KNOW HOW DAREDEVIL CAME TO *BE*.

THIS ISN'T YOUR *STYLE*. YOU'RE A *HITMAN*. NOT A *MASTER-MIND*.

YOU'D--BE--SURPRISED--HOW--INVENTIVE--A--MIND--CAN--BE--WHEN--IT--HAS--NOTHING--TO--DO--BUT--DREAM--OF--REVENGE.

I--RESEARCHED--YOUR--ORIGINS--

--RECRUITED--TEST--SUBJECTS--

--HIRED--CHEMISTS--

WHY NOT JUST *KILL* ME?

PLEASE. I--AM--IN--CONSTANT--ANGUISH--AND--TIME--PASSES--SO--SLOWLY.

THANKS--TO--YOU--EVERY--HOUR--OF--MY--EXISTENCE--IS--A--YEAR--

--EVERY--DAY--A--CENTURY.

WHY--WOULD--I--NOT--RETURN--THE--FAVOR?

"WHY--NOT--PROLONG--YOUR--TORTURE--

A.D.A. McDUFFIE

"--BY--STRIKING--WHERE--YOU--ARE--MOST--VULNERABLE?"

--JUST PLEASED THAT POOR MILLA FINALLY HAS ANY VISITOR AS LONG AS IT'S NOT MURDOCK.

HER EX-HUSBAND? THAT CREEP. HE'D BETTER NEVER COME AROUND, THE WAY HE BRINGS TROUBLE.

HE'LL BE THE DEATH OF HER.

I'LL ADMIT IT. NO POINT IN LYING IN FRONT OF A GOON WHO CAN HEAR MY HEARTBEAT.

YOU ALMOST HAD ME.

ALMOST.

THIS "GOON" WILL GIVE YOU TEN SECONDS TO EITHER ACT OR STAND DOWN--

SHUT UP.

YOU'RE IN NO POSITION TO MAKE DEMANDS.

NONE.

OH--MURDOCK--

--HOW--YOU--UNDERESTIMATE--ME.

LEVERAGE.

THAT'S--MY--ENDGAME. IT--ALWAYS--WAS.

YOU--WILL--ABANDON--YOUR--TOOTHLESS--THREAT--TO--MY--LIFE.

I--AM--DEAF--BUT--FOR--THIS--APPARATUS. I--AM--STRIPPED--OF--ALL--SENSES--SAVE--ONE.

ALL--I--HAVE--LEFT--ARE--MY--EYES.

ALL--I--WANT--IS--TO--SEE--YOU--DIE.

YOU--WILL--ENGAGE--IKARI--IN--FINAL--COMBAT.

AND--AS--YOU--DID--BEFORE----YOU--WILL--LOSE.

"OTHERWISE--ALL--THOSE--YOU--CARE--ABOUT--

"--ALL--THOSE--CLOSE--TO--YOU--

"--WILL--FALL--TO--SLAUGHTER.

"I--HAVE--PUT--NEAR--THEM--AGENTS--I--TRUST."

REALLY?

WELL...

...SO HAVE I.

CHKK

Bullseye.

Go. Go. Go.

Take every advantage.

Pull out every stop.

It all rides on this.

So give it everything.

Now that I've used up all my *sleight of hand*, though, I realize it's not *enough*.

Unlike *Ikari*, I'm *ragged*--running on *empty*.

I'm going to die after all.

And then it hits me.

A familiar *stench* from beneath the *floorboards.*

Snf

PAF

ZZZIP

CHAK

KASSHH

The smell of one last *Hail Mary.*

KRRSSH

The barrels and barrels of *chemicals* Bullseye used to create his *Daredevil knockoffs.*

Without breaking *stride,* I *lose* Ikari because he does exactly what I'm *counting* on him to do at the sight of what must be a hundred *hazardous waste* symbols.

Something I haven't done since I was a *kid.*

He *blinks.*

He's *faltering.* The air is filled with low-level radiation.

It clouds his radar sense with *static.*

He never sees me *coming.*

That, I hadn't counted on.

It's as if they're *choreographed*, these two. They should have worked together from the *start*.

They move like lightning.

TUNG

BLUNK

SLOOSH

The noise is so loud, it punches me in the *brain*.

A beat...two...and then, through the echoes, I hear something *tinny*, like the crackle of an old transistor radio.

--AAA-- AAHH-- AaAah--

And I realize I don't know what it sounds like when a man *drowns*.

"THERE WERE COPS AND EMTs ON THE SCENE ALMOST IMMEDIATELY--THAT *HAPPENS* IN NEW YORK WHEN A *BUILDING* COLLAPSES.

"THEY DRAGGED IKARI AND *LADY BULLSEYE* OUT OF THE RUBBLE AND STRAIGHT TO A MAXIMUM SECURITY FACILITY.

"I SUPPOSE BULLSEYE WILL FIND HIMSELF IN PRISON, AS WELL, BUT I'D CALL THAT REDUNDANT.

"YES, I GOT FREE AND PRIED HIM OUT OF THAT METAL TANK...

"...BUT NOT FAST ENOUGH TO SAVE HIS *SIGHT*."

NO EARS, NO EYES, NO WAY TO SMELL OR TASTE OR TOUCH...ONCE UPON A TIME, BULLSEYE WAS THE DEADLIEST MAN I'D EVER MET.

ALL HE'LL EVER BE *NOW* IS A LIVING BRAIN IN A FLESH-AND-BONE *COFFIN*.

HOW ARE *YOU*?

FUNNY MAN.

BOY, THE IRONY IS GENUINELY *STUPEFYING*.

BULLSEYE THOUGHT MAKING YOU *AFRAID*-- WHETHER FOR *YOURSELF* OR FOR YOUR *FRIENDS*--WOULD BE HIS *TRIUMPH*.

INSTEAD, IT *BACKFIRED*. BEING *SCARED* GAVE ME TIME TO *PLAN*.

DAD ALWAYS TAUGHT ME TO GET UP WHEN I'M KNOCKED DOWN. HE NEVER SAID I COULDN'T TAKE A SECOND IN *BETWEEN* TO *THINK*.

ONE LAST QUESTION. AS FAR AS I'M CONCERNED, THERE IS NO WRONG ANSWER, BUT YOU *WANT* TO *TELL* ME, SO I *WILL* ASK:

DID YOU *REALLY TRY* TO SAVE BULLSEYE FROM GOING BLIND?

MY NAME IS *FRANKLIN NELSON.* DAREDEVIL'S BEST FRIEND. I'M IN THE HOSPITAL FOR *CANCER.*

MY LIFE SUCKS.

PUNCHING CANCER

THEY'RE WAITING FOR YOU, MR. NELSON

≤SIGH≥

IT'LL BE GOOD FOR YOU *AND* THEM.

I'M NOT THE GUY FOR THIS, DR. FINE.

I WOULDN'T BE SO SURE. I'M NOT TERRIFIC WITH CHILDREN.

THE *LAST* TIME I BABYSAT, I LEARNED THE HARD WAY EXACTLY HOW MANY FIRE TRUCKS THERE ARE IN QUEENS.

YOU'RE NOT BABYSITTING. YOU'RE SPEAKING TO A *GROUP.*

SURELY A *TRIAL LITIGATOR* CAN DO THAT WITH EASE. BESIDES, YOU PROMISED. AND IT GETS YOU OUT OF BED.

YOU KNOW HOW KIDS ARE. THEY HAVE A BILLION QUESTIONS, ESPECIALLY ABOUT *SUPER HEROES.*

WHY AREN'T THEY JUST ASKING *IRON MAN?*

BECAUSE HE'S NOT YET *ARRIVED,* AND THEY KNOW THAT *YOU'VE* MET THE FANTASTIC FOUR AND SUB-MARINER AND GOD KNOWS WHO ELSE.

CELEBRITY BY *ASSOCIATION.*

I'VE BEEN THEIR *LAWYER.* WE DON'T *HANG OUT.*

RUMOR HAS IT YOU KNOW *DAREDEVIL* QUITE WELL.

THEY'LL WANT TO HEAR ABOUT HIM, *TOO.*

TRUST ME, YOU'LL DO FINE. IT'S *NOT* A BIG *DEAL.*

WHAT ARE THEY WORKING ON?

A *GIFT* for Iron Man. They're writing and drawing a *COMIC BOOK* for him.

IT WAS *THEIR* IDEA. QUITE *CHARMING*--

BZZZT BZZZT

OH, MY.

I'M LATE FOR A *CONSULT.* TELL THE NURSE IF YOU NEED ANYTHING.

I DO! A GOOD STORY ABOUT THE *FANTASTIC FOUR* OR THE *SUB-MARINER!*

YOU'RE *LEAVING* ME HERE?

YOU'LL DO GREAT. RELAX.

...THEN *BA-ZAM!*

HAHA!

HULK *SMASH!*

HEY, THIS SOUNDS LIKE A FUN PROJECT.

CAN I *SEE?*

SHOW HIM!

IT'S THE AVENGERS, AND THEY'RE IN, LIKE, THIS *GINORMOUS* FIGHT!

AGAINST THE DIS... ...DISINTEG... DISINTEGROSAURUS!

I GOT AN IDEA! *GIMME!*

HOLY COW, THE *IMAGINATION* IN THESE KIDS.

AND THE ENERGY. WHERE DOES *THAT* COME FROM?

...AN' THEN... AN' THEN... *WOLVERINE* GOES ALL *NINJA* ON HIM!

HE NEEDS *NINJA* ARMOR!

HE WOULD LOOK *SO COOL* WITH NINJA ARMOR!

THEY'RE PATIENTS IN A CANCER WARD, FOR HEAVEN'S SAKE. I'M PRETTY DOWN ABOUT MY SITUATION, BUT *THEY* HAVE BEEN DEALT A *HORRIBLE* HAND.

SOME ARE HERE FOR DAYS. SOME FOR *MONTHS.*

SOME UNTIL THE END.

...AND THEN IRON MAN SAYS, *"LOOK OUT, SPIDER-MAN!"*

BUT THEY'RE NOT DWELLING ON THAT.

THEIR *TOTAL FOCUS* IS ON *THIS.*

EVERYONE PITCHES IN... *EVERY KID...*

I BET *CAPTAIN AMERICA* WOULD HIT THE DISINTEGROSAURUS WITH HIS *SHIELD!*

IT COMES *BACK* TO HIM LIKE A *BOOMERANG!*

...EVEN THE ONES WHO CAN'T GO TWENTY MINUTES WITHOUT THROWING UP.

TAKE THAT, YOU *MONSTER!*

THIS IS *AWESOME.*

THEY EXPLAIN TO ME THE BEAST IS CALLED *"DISINTEGROSAURUS"* BECAUSE ITS *TOUCH* AND ITS *FLAME-BREATH* MAKE THINGS WEAK.

WITHER *TREES,* TURN BUILDINGS TO *DUST,* THAT SORT OF THING.

FOR A SECOND, THE KIDS PLOT THEMSELVES INTO A *CORNER,* SO I PITCH IN.

HOW ABOUT THIS IS WHERE *DAREDEVIL* COMES IN? HE CAN USE HIS *BILLY CLUB* TO--

DAREDEVIL? *HULK!*

YEAH, *HULK! HULK SMASHES!*

SMASH

HULK BRING FRIEND.

URRM, THANK YOU, *HULK!*

IT IS *I,* MR. FANTASTIC! AVENGERS ASSEMBLE!

I'VE JUST LEARNED THE DISINTEGROSAURUS IS AN ESCAPEE FROM AN *EXPERIMENTAL LAB!*

HIS POWERS COME FROM A *SUPER-CANCER* THAT GOT SPLICED INTO HIS DNA!

THEN I'LL ADJUST THE SETTINGS ON MY *GAUNTLET--*

TIK TAK

VVVVRRRR

--AND BATHE HIM IN A SPECIAL ANTI-CANCER BEAM!

IT'S WORKING! HE'S RETURNING TO NORMAL!

HE WON'T BE A THREAT ANYMORE, AVENGERS!

BURP

MY ARMOR CAN DO ANYTHING! USING MY SPECIAL ULTRA-ZAP FREQUENCIES, I'VE CURED 'SAURY OF HIS CONDITION!

HE'LL BE JUST FINE NOW!

AVENGERS!

GIANT-MAN? THERE ARE *MORE* MUTATED DISINTEGROSAURS BUSTING UP P.S. 462! WE HAVE TO GO FIX *THEM,* TOO!

CLEVER. DINOSAURS INFECTED WITH "SUPER-CANC--"

--OH--

--OH, *NO...*

THESE KIDS.

THEY'RE MAKING THIS STORY FOR IRON MAN TO *READ.*

THEY THINK HE CAN CURE *CANCER.*

THEY THINK HE CAN CURE *THEM.*

OH, *GOD.*

UMM... GUYS? I...I KNOW YOU'RE EXCITED, BUT YOU SHOULD...

...BEFORE IRON MAN GETS HERE AND THIS GETS TOO *FAR,* YOU SHOULD... KNOW THAT...

...

...SUPER HEROES CAN DO A WHOLE LOT, BUT THEY...

...THEY CAN'T CURE CANCER.

DUH. IT'S A *COMIC BOOK.*

EXCUSE ME--

WELCOME IRON MAN

SUPERHEROES LOVE US

--BUT I WAS TOLD I'D FIND SOME MIGHTY BRAVE CHILDREN IN THIS ROOM!

IS THAT TRUE?

YAY, IRON MAN!

IT'S HIM! IT'S HIM!

IRONNNN MANNNNN!

EXCELLENT! I KNEW HE WOULDN'T LET THEM DOWN!

HOW DID IT GO, MR. NELSON?

SORT OF BAFFLINGLY, DOC. THIS COMIC THEY CAME UP WITH...

WELCOME IRON MAN

...IS EXCELLENT THERAPY, WOULDN'T YOU AGREE?

THEY REALIZE IT'S FANTASY...?

OF COURSE. KIDS ARE SMART. THEY KNOW WHAT'S FACT AND WHAT'S FICTION.

BUT THEIR HEROES ARE *REAL*, AND THESE BOYS AND GIRLS LOOK TO *THEM* FOR *INSPIRATION* AND FOR *STRENGTH*. THEY LONG TO *IDENTIFY* WITH THEM.

IF THEY STAND *ANY* CHANCE OF SURVIVAL, THEY HAVE TO BELIEVE THEIR CONDITION CAN BE *BATTLED*, CAN BE *BEATEN*--

--AND IF IMAGINING THE *HULK* PUNCHING CANCER RIGHT IN THE *FACE*, OR *WHATEVER*--

--IF *THAT'S* WHAT GETS THEIR BLOOD RACING AND KINDLES THEIR *FIGHTING SPIRIT*, I'LL *TAKE* IT.

DO YOU UNDERSTAND, MR. NELSON?

POW

... YEAH.

END

TWENTY-FIVE MANY ARMORS OF IRON MAN
VARIANT BY JORGE MOLINA

TWENTY-FIVE

VARIANT BY ADAM KUBERT, DANNY MIKI & JUSTIN PONSOR

TWENTY-SIX **VARIANT BY PAOLO RIVERA**

DD readers—

I thought we'd take a couple pages to show some of the behind the scenes work that Mark and Chris do to make Daredevil such a compelling read each month. Hope you like it!

—SW

DAREDEVIL #26
SCRIPT FOR 20 PAGES/MARCH 11-25, 2013

PAGE SIXTEEN through SEVENTEEN

(However you think it paces out best, Chris!)

PANEL: A MINUTE LATER. MATT, IN A DOCTOR'S COAT, SNEAKS PAST SOME OTHERWISE-OCCUPIED NURSES AT THE NURSES' STATION--

DD CAPTION: First step: duck out of the crosshairs.

DD CAPTION: Ikari's no doubt tracking my every move the same way I would HIS:

DD CAPTION: By listening for the distinctive HEARTBEAT of his PREY.

PANEL: --AND STEALS SEVERAL SYRINGES MARKED "ADRENALINE."

DD CAPTION: I can't stop my pulse, nor can I mute it.

DD CAPTION: But I can CHANGE it.

PANELS: A MOMENT LATER, MATT'S WALKING SWIFTLY THROUGH THE EMERGENCY ROOM--LOTS AND LOTS OF HEARTBEATS ALL AROUND, INCLUDING HIS OWN HEARTLINE, CENTRAL--

--IKARI, IN A HOODIE, IS FOLLOWING HIM, TRACKING HIS HEARTBEAT--

--AND, UNNOTICED IN ALL THE CHAOS AND COMMOTION, MATT REMOVES THREE ADRENALINE SYRINGES FROM HIS DOCTOR'S COAT POCKET--

--AND JAMS THEM INTO HIS CHEST, SENDING HIS PULSERATE SOARING--

--BLENDING IN WITH ALL THE OTHER HEARTBEATS AS MATT DIVES THROUGH A THICK CROWD, IKARI IN PURSUIT--

--AND IKARI BREAKS THROUGH THE CROWD, A CACOPHONY OF OVERLAPPING HEARTLINES--AND NO SIGN OF MATT!

((more))

After all the inked art is in, Javier prepares "color flats" keeping in mind the setting and mood of the scene. When this is done he creates the final, rendered color.

DAREDEVIL #26/Script/Ms. Page 2   MARK WAID

PAGES SIXTEEN through SEVENTEEN, continued

PANEL: BARKING INTO A CELLPHONE, IKARI TAKES OFF RUNNING INTO A
NEARBY ALLEYWAY.

IKARI: It's ME. Murdock took himself OFF THE GRID.

IKARI: I don't KNOW how!

PANEL: FROM A LOW ROOFTOP, HE LOOKS DOWN HELPLESSLY, SEES
NOTHING OF NOTE.

IKARI: Probably to his APARTMENT. His OFFICE. Someplace
                PRIVATE, without CANNON FODDER around.

PANEL: CUT TO LADY BULLSEYE IN THE CLOCK TOWER ON THE PHONE, AT
THE OTHER END OF THE CALL.

PHONE/elec: Tell me how you wish me to proceed.

Mark and Chris work so closely together that the scripts can go from very detailed to very loose depending on the scene. Chris usually knows how to nail EXACTLY what Mark is looking for.

IKARI SLOWED BY A STRETCHER   LOST HIM!

SCRIPT SAYS ALLEY BUT THAT FEELS TOO ABRUPT

production: irene y. lee